LUMINESCENT ON THE INSIDE

Poetry From Within

KAREN LANGRAN

LUMINESCENT ON THE INSIDE

POETRY FROM WITHIN

By Karen Langran

Transcendent Publishing
PO Box 66202
St. Pete Beach, FL 33736
www.TranscendentPublishing.com

Transcendent
Publishing

ISBN: 978-0-9993125-8-2

Printed in the United States of America

DEDICATION

Dedicated to my loving husband, Rory

and

My beautiful daughters, Sofia and Aurora.

Life is illuminated in all directions with your love and support.

CONTENTS

ACKNOWLEDGMENTS

To Sue & PAS, my two rocks...you know not what you have taught me and continue to do so. Thank you so much! Love you both.

To Marsha, for your guidance and words of wisdom over the years.

To My Daughters, Sofia and Aurora, I love you both with all my heart and am honored to be your Mom.

To My Husband, Rory, there are no words for your constant support, patience, love and commitment. I love you very much.

To Transcendent Publishing...thank you for the opportunity once again, and the belief in me.

"Let my burdens be lifted on the wings of an angel and be gone."

Quote by Karen Langran 8/19/2017

To My Readers,

I will continue to reach down deep and grow internally, spiritually and else. My goal is to bring some peace to my soul, but learning a little bit of vulnerability along the way by sharing my ideas with the world, because why not? Who says you have to be a celebrity to be right or know everything or get a reward or even to reach your own goals?! I would never imagine that the lessons will end, but rather keep on coming at me in rapid fire. I am constantly learning to protect myself and it is tiring.

The release of words, communication, and another language has ALWAYS intrigued me, back to when I started learning Italian and realized that I could say everything differently and still be understood. It was empowering to have multiple choices, even if I was only bilingual. So why does one forget about their dreams and goals? I will tell you, life gets in the way. People and situations stop you dead in your tracks and you can't figure it out. You are swayed in time and your dreams no longer matter. You think you are not good enough and that no one will care. So you let your dreams blow in the wind and fly away.

Well, at some point in life, after being beaten down, you realize you are important just like everyone else, just like God intended for you. So you decide to come out of your shell and take a chance, a moment created by you. But again, traumas, disappointments, deaths, injustices all get in the way. You are part of something bigger, but if you don't stay grounded within yourself, you will become lost again.

You have to realize that your one small difference may not reach the world, but aren't we a sum of its parts? So if you reach your own inner circle, your spouse, your daughter, your son, your friend, a teacher, then it should matter. It should matter because one person was reached and you never knew it, but you simplified things and did it for you, and in the process someone was helped along the way. That is strength from within. If no one was helped but you, then that matters too, for you are important in this world. You have a purpose, a job to do, a moment in time to create memories and bring your dreams to fruition. So shine in this light and your world will stay luminescent from within.

Thanks so much for taking this journey with me. If your path shall cross mine, I hope it will bring light and love to you and me.

Kindly,
Karen

THE DIVINE
Dedicated to Grandma T.

Two halves make a whole
Two vines bring you home
One branch supports it all.

One to the other
    Connected by the divine
Bouncing balls of light
Transferring the energy
    held within.
Exchanging thoughts
Memories of fun.
Intertwining vines
    that grow
    moving every day
Water to make it grow
Tears to move it along
All the time meandering
    down a path that doesn't show.
Two parts of a whole
    That's <u>me</u> and <u>you</u>
    Divine.
Divide your time so you will know
    How to make your time move slow.
Find a way to grow and grow.
Branch out
    And walk tenderly
Balancing between the here and now
Knowing you can make it somehow.

Don't get whisked away by the wind
    You know we have all sinned.

But gingerly proceed
So you can reach out a hand
And pull
The branch will not break.
It does not need to be straight.
    Curves to gather strength
    Bends to hold on tight
    Notches to keep you right.
Two halves make up a whole
And I know
    You and me
    Will not sever
    Divine is forever

Guided by the light
An everlasting sight
Sparks pull you there
    It isn't fair.

Think it all out.
Like a reel in a film.
Two vines jutting out.
    Do not trip
    I will shout
Connects you there
    And all about
Just trying to settle in.
    To a place I like to be

While I simply look out
    upon my windowsill
And gaze at the sun so bright
    Then it turns into a
    star-filled night.
Leaving me mesmerized
    At the divine light.

Let it happen in due time
There really is no worry
So plant your feet
    Upon your seat
Reaching high
Up at the sky
While stars keep on coming by.
For you are one, made up of two
Just waiting for God to see
    you through
    to the other side.
You will slide upon that branch
with all its twists and turns
Gaining speed up on ahead.

Until you find the
    Hands of the Divine.

Hands that support
Hearts that care
Bring you back
If you dare.

LAYERS

Layers
Look deep inside to a new start
Even if the outer layer is all ragged
Twists and turns abide
Sometimes the corner is just ahead
Stop, start, gouge it out again
Pick one layer off and see what is inside
You might just be surprised.
Sustain the music while you can
Joy is never found outside, but rather deep within the layers
You will find
A sense of peace, an escape into the moment, a happiness like no other
Self-love is here, just give it a chance to thrive.
When all is said and done, there will still be layers to drop, peel, grow anew
Until you are thoroughly through
But when you get to the ultimate layer inside, there is goodness and light and warmth
And God will guide you through.
Layers all around...the fakeness of a smile, having a bad day, putting up a layer to protect your good deep inside.
What if we took those layers and turned them inside out?
What would we find?
Could you imagine the happiness?

> The pretentiousness shedding, the fake smiles coming to a halt, the walls crumbling down. Perhaps a genuine caring would abide all around, picking others up and trying one more time.

Start your day inside out and play to your true feelings.
Let the world shine together in sharing the happiness deep inside

the layers,
Your layers, giving back to the world and allowing your layers to shine.
What if we painted those layers to make them fresh again?...In jewel tones so the effervescence is amazing...and curved one layer to the next to create your own story...and weaved around someone else's layers to create a harmony like no other...would it create a majestic loom of history?
A layer of quilted stories to allow oneself to laugh in the moment, to bring forth the magical memories of time. Swip-swap some of these layers and see what you will find.
Share in the staggering stories of life and just be.
No expectations, no fear, no anxiety...just be.
Layer it on thick and bring it home with you.
For when you layer those good things on, the moment opens up to immense proportions.
The world shines in a new light.
The layers look appealing and full of color.
Perspective anew, you tread out into the world with a sense of possibility, a pride like no other, for you are ready to pile on the new layers from the inside-out.
Layers just waiting for you.

CONSTANT RUSH OF PANIC

Constant Rush of Panic
That gnawing feeling inside
Wondering how to get out, where to turn, if the walls will close in
and crush you
Not sure if you should flee
Or find a space outside to just be
Get some fresh air before you panic
Take a breath to ground you
In your head find some sense... it is not there
You cannot find any peace from this constant rush of panic
Anxious feelings abide
Swell up inside of you
Churning and turning for a way out
A way out. Go this way, not that
Move over, not here
Stay in place, not meander
Render it all useless
Keep it going in your head
Find a way to stay within
Because when you truly sense the big picture,
You simply want to turn around and go home
There is a lot of energy swirling around
Permeating the air you breathe
Contaminating all that you worked to clean
Is it worth the battle, the battle to stay safe
Free from the work and strength it takes to mingle
Jingle along like the others
Try to fit in
Find a smooth feature to focus on
Truly it has to work, why not for me?
This constant rush of panic

Ready to flee
An exorbitant amount of pressure
To experience the world
Fake it till you make it
Beauty is on the outside
Stillness lies within, your real worth
See through all the smoke
And make it to the other side
For freedom to see, breathe and do will help you through
Stand tall and straight
Pretend you have a date with those around you
Just show up and with luck
You will make it through
For your heart is pushing you
To try with all your might
And see anew in your eyes
The light that is guiding you to the top
The top of the branch to take hold of
Teetering on the edge of time
Running on fumes
Hoping beyond hope that this constant rush of panic will subside.

THE BOND

The Bond
Intertwining circular paths
Holding on tight
Let the magic flow
Isn't it nice to have this trust?
A way to care and share in complete security
One leaves the circle of trust and you must quickly close up the gap
No way to glue it or patch it
Some bonds are more sturdy and dependable than others
These are the real ones.
No fakeness abounds
No making excuses.
True joy in helping one another
True caring in what you do and say
All in order to help another you love
This sense of peace and trust overflow your heart
It expands to create more
A deeper understanding of all that has passed
An excitement of being together
And a yearning to create a much brighter future
The bond is circular in nature
When one is up, the other is down
When one has needs, the other one gives
When one is hurt, the other one dries their tears
But mostly, the bond is unbreakable with only a few rules
Never betray
Bending down to help is a must
No egos allowed
Kind and simple honesty is the key
Avoiding conflicts does not work
It simply breaks the bond to shreds

Making one distrust the other
Never a way to mend
Create new rules when one arrives
But never forget who you are and why you are here
Memories are solid
Important to create
Essential to staying alive,
For in making and preserving memories, one knows who they
really are
Trusting the other with their open souls
Knowing they have your back
And keeping the kids along for the ride
Wonder why that happens
Why kids get lost in the shuffle
Perhaps it is because someone does not think the bond is essential
But little do they know that bond was forever
And forever doesn't mean you ignore what is right and choose
what is more fun
Doing things for yourself without harming others is the key to the
unbreakable bond
And not knocking those to the wayside
Especially those who care and have loved you forever
Pulling the rug out from under you is not kind.
It is cruel. It is deliberate.
You know what you are doing, but you do not want to stop.
It does not matter anymore.
It tears you up inside and you let it.
Swells your heart with pride and ego,
Better take a step back and decide if this feeling is worth it
Unbreakable bonds...they can be broken...especially by one
One who refuses to back down
And communicate anymore
Wants to go out the door
And forget what has happened
What was created in love and kindness for that essential bond to

even start
Has long been forgotten by you
And you do not care.
The kids are to suffer from the choices you made
Seems a long way to go down in a ditch
A canyon, not a crevice
Only time will tell
Will you let go of the hideousness?
Or will you continue with the happiness of the flesh?
The heart will break and mend,
But it will leave behind those who no longer matter
Like you
Who has decided to put your family memories aside
And pack them away in your heart
And choose to put in someone new
One with no bonds at all
One that cannot even fall
One with a pompousness so deep
It cannot even be dug out and removed.
It's ok to try something new
But not at the expense of others
That is not true.
Leave your ego unchecked and that is what happens
You soar high above the others
Thinking you are better than them
You think you know more,
But instead you are at the door
Burdened by all those who look about
And refuse to see it out
The bond is already broken
No need for excuses now
You chose your path,
A broken one
And one that ignores others along the way
Guess it was not meant anyway.

SEEDS PLANTED

Seeds of Doubt
Once a seed of doubt is planted, it is hard to trust again
For that tiny speck of doubt lights up like a siren
Leading you to question all that is in front of you

But if you can turn that tiny speck of doubt around,
That seed of doubt
Can turn to a very small seed of hope.

Seeds of Hope
Glimmer with fairy dust,
Hoping beyond imaginable boundaries
Ready to set out again
Try again
New adventures, new beginnings
No endings, for there is hope

Seeds of hope can grow and grow
Can come to fruition in your mind first
Then ever so slowly,
Seeds of hope gather speed and momentum
Making friends along the way
Opening up to...

Supporting one another
Seeing the future
Investing in your strength
A feeling of togetherness
Seeds of hope bring out the passion,
The drive, the colors once again.

Seeds of Change
Beyond the doubt,
Beyond the hope,
There is change...
Seeds of change

Seeds of change
Help you to see beyond the veil,
Pick up scattered wrongdoings along the way
Brings about hope infinitum

Seeds of change
Leaves the past alone
Brings forth the now
Prepares you for what lies ahead
So you can absorb the changes around you
And free yourself from the bonds of doubt
And live in the world of hope once again

So the universe can spark a change that is seen from the ground to
the heavens
And those seeds will actually take hold and plant in someone else's
mind
To take hold, to take shape, to actually grow the change that is
needed

Seeds of Doubt,
Lead to
Seeds of Hope,
Lead to
Seeds of Change.

Be the Change.

LUMINESCENCE

Luminescence
Shining forth a brilliant light
Sparkles all around
Tiny crystals of light
Seek and you shall find

How to find a way through the dark
No one ever knows
Bring a friend
And they will lend
Helping you to grow

Slow at first
Until you thirst
For the essence of the light
Imagine bright
It won't bite
See it through the dark night

Wind around
Not a sound
You will soon be found
And brought forth
Upon the ground
While little lights soon grow

Burning bright
Into the night
Like diamonds on the snow
Pick them up and throw
They will jump and glow

Luminescence
A pinprick of light
Waiting to be bright
So it will soon create
A halo of essence
Lessen it will not
For then you will surely rot

Light does not need a street
For when you meet
It will glow and grow
Into a space
Ready to race
Pick up the pace
It is nearly dawn

Look out upon the lawn
Pearls aglow
Shining in delight
Bursting with newness
Accepting nothing less
Patiently aglow

Close your eyes
The light shines on
Through each and every lash
Make a bigger stash
For when you need it
It will fit

Meandering about
Until it comes shining through
To take you through
The new steps of the day

Teaching you to play
Maybe next time you will stay
And quietly pray

For the light shines bright
To remind you day and night
As you strut about your day
And lay unto your bed
Turn on your light
Keep it shining
A brilliance so strong
You cannot go wrong

For when a light is strong
It can help another
A fellow brother
And not lead you astrother
Balancing between the right and wrong

Luminescence
A brilliance sparkling outward
No need to tamp it down
Let it through
Come on you
Another dawn is here

Have no fear
See its light shine through.
And all the world will grow
For you took a chance
And shared the brewing stew
Of everything that is you.

JEWELS OF CONTEMPLATION

Jewels of Contemplation
Powerful intentional thoughts
Coming together as a whole
Fragments of the mind working non-stop
Trying to make sense of its parts
Filling in the holes with positivity and direction
Creating a reality of colorful vibrance
Connecting the here and now to its thoughts
Just passing through...

Jewels of contemplation
An array of colors, shining like a rainbow
Bringing in the light
Combining it with the shadows
And filling the dark holes with hope
Astral planing at its best

Jewels of contemplation
Allowing you to become one with the jewels of light
Turn it around and catch a new angle
Play it through in your mind
Perspective changes
Clears the air
Allows the thoughts to flow again
Energy unstuck
Coming at you in torrents
Quick as a lightning rod

STUCK IN A BASEMENT

In a basement of a building
Stairs after stairs turning around
No way out
Exits blocked
Hard cold gray concrete
Metal doors clanging shut
Pulling them open one last time
Trying to get to the outside air
Go right, go left, back up, then down again.
Too many nooks and crannies
Not much time
Do I go up another flight?
Will I find my way out?
Sit down, give up
Rest awhile
Get up, hunker down
Think awhile
Follow the light
Is there any light peeking through these doors?
Gotta get out of here
No windows
Can't look out
Look up
Find some help
Breathe
Smell the air
Breathe
One door opens, pull, pulling hard
It's stuck, pull harder
Got it!
Out, I have no idea where I am
But I can breathe again.
Let it out and cry.

SUSPENDED THOUGHTS

Thoughts suspended in space and time
Surround us at every corner
Energetically swirling without a care
You can't take it back
It is out there for all to see
Relish in the good thoughts
Ban the negative ones
For you never know who is looking
Make them your own thoughts, not to let them out
For this is how you must secure
Your own life in a protective bubble
Circle around it
Say what you want
But thoughts are suspended in space and time
Bring the good ones closer to last
Don't let the sad ones tear you apart
And don't let the mad ones rip you in pieces
For thoughts are things
And things become words
And words are actions
And actions become behaviors
And behaviors are habits
And habits become you.
So if you don't like your thoughts suspended in space and time
Bring them inside for a chance to chat
Stew and brew
Until your thoughts
Become the life of you.

CARVED OUT OF STONE
Dedicated to Rory

Carved Out of Stone
Everlasting love
Side by side
Deeply rooted
Sustained by a single thread that reaches out into infinity
Weaving the web of humanity
Creating a family
Longevity at its finest
"Unto dust you shall return"
Completing the life cycle
Grappling with the ups and downs of life itself
This connective thread continues to pull you along
Showing you the way
Abundant choices ahead
Creating a world all your own
Ride it with someone else
Marriage is a bond
One that lasts forever in your heart and soul
Sealing the fates of time
Realizing all that you have
And keeping it close to your heart
Mindful of the bumps along the road
Quietly trudging along, with your partner
Waiting for them to catch up
Pulling the energy together
Making it flow faster and smoother
Riding the waves of life
Feeling buoyant and free
Energy connecting
So that you are deeply rooted

Side by side
Inside out
And all around
Caring deeply, shining brilliantly
Reaching the vastness of space
Molding your moments
Imaginations wild, without end
Sustaining your love
Through and through.

REJOICE IN NATURE

Strong
Glittering, shimmery light peeking through your eyelids
Open them, see all there is to see
Find and discover the strength of the universe
Trying to project its messages on you
       Be it an arch of greenery on top of a pagoda
       Tall cypress flanking its sides
       Colorful flowers blooming around
       Precious fruit ripening on the vine
       Cheerful birds singing a tune
       Dog exploring new scents on the ground
In the air, a mixture of newness and fresh spring air
Breezes blowing to cool your skin
Kindness abounds in nature like no other

But don't get it mad because she can do frightful things
Weather patterns change abruptly
Storms coming in to cloud your view
Raindrops pounding to the ground
Changing your plans on a dime

A chill in the air is refreshing
Try to see through the storm
Like waves of an ocean, ever-changing its direction
Rising and falling to match the rhythm of the earth
Enjoy the thunderous sounds
Droplets of salty water cascading down
Finding a new place to rest

Return to your day...
Refreshed,
Renewed,
Rebalanced.

And Rejoice.

PARTS & PIECES

Parts and pieces of me
A world swirling with kindness
Please let me in
The injustices of it all, in a world so small
Do not judge, do not care
Fare

Notes

Breath of light
Take it all in
Night to refresh
Replenish your sources
Talk to your head
Your mind matters
Your heart above it all
Fun somewhere in between

Vulnerable to others
So they may understand you
And you may make some new trusted friends
Why you say?
Because it is lonely if you do not play
Reach for the stars
Don't let them walk all over you

Ideas

Stand up for what you believe in
Take a stand
Until you find a purposeful soul

Wear your courage
Inside and out
Bring it to the others in need
What is it that you will find?
Deep inside

A place of security
Safe from all harm
Only a mother can bring that comfort
But if she does not exist,
You can create a love everlasting
One that is only you and God
For God will never abandon you
Not your heart, nor your mind, nor your soul
He will lift you up in places you see as dismal
And bring you peace to be found
Surrender to the Source
The Light, the Divine to lift you up high
To further your stance of caring
Sharing in a way that is unselfish
Not doing it for you
Always remembering where you come from

Lengthening the shadows all around
Whispers to get you there
Bring about a change
Like a gentle nudging
A breeze pushing you along the right path
Listening to your gut
Intuition
Believe it
See it
Catch it

Why?
How does one simply let go?
Can you believe a mother could be so indulgent?
So cruel to even suck the life right out of you?
Not a mother I want to be
One that doesn't learn her life lessons
Keeps on doing it for her
With no remorse to those around her
She will do it all alone
For she has abandoned those she used to love
Was it all fake?
Did she simply use us?
Does she only care about offspring?
How does one go from completely free and kind
To one of closed doors, sheltered by manipulation
Egos unchecked
Bringing about hate and beyond cruel
She knows what she does
She does it willingly, without a care
Bringing about hatred,
Actual hate
Actual distaste and non-caring
Broken, never to be repaired
Torn at the seams
She created it
She knows what she is doing

No one can bring her back
God sees her intentions
All for the life force of physical pleasure
One that is conniving, manipulative,
Unable to grow and expand
Only for himself
Only to be roped in by his control

Believing it is for "family"
But he is so "uncomfortable"
So let's ditch this joint
No one will notice
No one will care

Only those that used to love
But no longer feel
Their hearts and souls ripped out
Once again
To show the world that some people
Are simply evil, simply unkind,
Tend to get their way when strangling another
Under the guise of hope and promise
Under the "story" of poor me
A fakeness so thick you could put a match to it
And up in flames it would go
Smoke carrying him to another evil path
For someone else to follow
Until you have exhausted all your ways
And those strangled have lost their footing
A path keep following until it dead ends
But those left behind are out of love now
Out of hope
Never wanting to reconcile
Wanting to simply cut the bonds forever
Remembering how it used to be so simple
How it used to be tethered to love
Now holding on to hate
A hiatus of hate
A break of love, of all bonds good

No one asks for a break from their daughter
No one does that
There is a reason
A hateful man who is in control
One who is so shrewd he comes in slowly for the kill
Creeps up so fast and tight it doesn't show any trails
But those close to the victim see it all
They see it happening in steps
They see it swirling around
They taste the uneasiness in the air
They hear the underhanded comments of hatred, jealously, being
left out
Poor me
Poor unhappy me
Wrap your arms around a facade
And that is what you will get
Another facade with a hole so big
It blows you by
It creeps up and poof
You are gone
From those you loved
Those you lived for
And those you cared for
No longer.

Ripped from the womb as they say
Taken from the tomb
Chiseled from the family
Together no more
Pieces and chunks never to grow back together.
Pasted and taped no more.

Used to belong together. Sewn in at so many levels,
Brought about by Time and Love.
She has forgotten those two words,
Time and Love.
Those used to be the crux of her soul.
The way she used to live her life.
But now love only matters in a fake way, with only one.
Does that even make sense?
And time does not matter.
For time is a game to her
And she thinks age is time
And time is aging.
And if you are older, there is no time left,
So push those to the wayside and see what happens
Well you become a hill of one
A mountain alone
With one man to push you off when he reaches the top
"Over the top" is what she calls it
Maybe she sees that in him and wants to blame me
Why would she admit fault or blame?
It would not suit her or him.
It would slow them down
And "time is precious"
And when you run out of time,
You wish you had it back
And when you refuse to listen
Or give an inch
Or budge a thought
Or even grab a friend
You will lose because you have already lost
You have lost and ignored
Those you loved
Those who truly cared
Those who made a difference

And you have chosen
To be on your own
For selfish purposes
For ego-maniacs
For controlling freaks
For social misfits
For conniving creatures of habit
All for a purpose that you haven't found yet in yourself
Never accepting the consequences
Never looking back to who you have run over
Never caring to even glance in the rear view mirror

And never getting back the time spent on love
The time spent on grieving
The time spent on repairing your soul
The ones that lifted you up
To another realm
So you could get some fresh air
So you could truly breathe again
No, you said
You need "a break"
A "hiatus"
One that is never-ending
One that you can control at your leisure
Well time does not wait nor stop for anyone
And your choices are running out of time
And you cannot get that back
The kids keep on growing and learning
They are learning the feel of abandonment
Of letting go
Of knowing that love can change overnight
That goodness can turn into evil
That people "can change"
And that those that made promises can break them

Parents are not supposed to do that
They are supposed to help you find the light,
They are supposed to love you unconditionally
But not my mom
She has chosen the wrong way
A path so rocky and broken
She will never find her way back
She will simply trod on
Trample on all that she has built
For a crazy man
One that is selfish, hateful, unkind
And the worst one there ever was
All because she lost and didn't grieve fully
For when she lost big
She thought he could be replaced
But she was wrong
No one is ever replaced
For God only made One of each of us
So that we are each unique
And some have chosen the Other Way
Some have chosen to stray
Away from all that is and ever was
Taking any weak ones along the way
Taking the vulnerable ones
Returning them to a pathway of destruction
An evil, rocky path that cannot be reversed
For one never forgets what you did along the way
One simply cannot forget the trouble you caused
The sorrow
The stress
Turning our souls inside out
Ripping the seams sewn together through time
No more tethered together
No strings attached
Clearly braving it another way

Seeming to work out for your ego,
But lost so many along the way
Guess it is not important now
For you chose to go away
And that includes the best of us
The light has gone out
And no one is no longer home.

COMING IN FOR THE KILL

Coming in for the Kill
Swooping down
Upon the ground
Stalking, lurking around
Ssshh, not a sound
And you will not be found

You think you know me
And then you don't
You are no longer free
Don't you See?

Soundless
Airless
Don't breathe a word
You think you are heard

In fact you are not family
You are a stranger
Danger to all
Making you fall
Over the edge

Into an abyss
So deep
So steep
There is no turning back
Or you will get flack
From the stranger
Who cares not
He wants what you got

Think you can outrun him?
Think again.
And then...
He is one step ahead of you
And you are through

When you turn down that path
Slowly you are last
All of it is in the past
But you must think fast

See who has been lost along the way
Ask them to stay
Maybe they will get help
So be loud and yelp
Dig deep and be heard
Listen and you will find
That others have stumbled and fell

But they accepted the thoughts
The advice along the way
And they chose to stay
Hidden in the path of hurt
Giving you their last shirt
Wanting you to wait up
And fill your cup
With the breath of hope
That you will change your ways

And not continue with a stranger
That is clear and present danger
Who wants you to fall
So he can chuckle through it all
And get what he wants

Not a care in the world
What's in it for him?

In the meantime
You have severed all the lines
That allows you to find your way back
Out of the pack of wolves
Who will gladly eat you up
And leave you stuck
Upon a path of destruction

Leaving you at a crossroads
One where you can take off a load
Either find yourself again
Or blocked by a dead end

Your choice
Your life
Friend to find
Or stranger to bring you to danger

Your heart
Your mind
Use it or lose it
Gut intuition
Steers you away
Will not lead you astray

Trust it
Leave it
Love it, your life
No more strife

ABANDONMENT TO ENLIGHTENMENT

Abandonment
Enlightenment tea
Water rolling over the rocks
Cascading down freely
Tinkling around the pebbles in its way
Brushing aside any dirt, any fear, any doubt
Sweeping aside the worries, the darkness
Allowing light to seep in to the crevices
A pinprick of light expanding
Extending out to reach the sky
Meeting the heavens along the way

Oceans meeting the shoreline
Abrupt crashing of the waves on the sand
Petering out as it draws back
Leaving a frothy white foam behind
Again, a thunderous roar
A crash like no other
God-like, but not commanding
Full, but not scary
Prompting you to run in it and play
Or sink into the sand and stay

As it settles in for the night
A stillness so deep
Blackness is hovering above, waiting to ascend down
All around and bathe one with its coat
Then the moon takes its stance above
Guarding so the ocean can sleep

Shining like a beacon to protect the waters below
The waves become rhythmic
Timed to its "breathing"
Restoring energy for another night

Waking up fully refreshed to play
Entertaining crowds with its spray
Sounds no longer muted
Gaining speed and momentum
Crashing upon the shore
Ready for more

Castles built upon my floor
Hours of wonderment and glee
Toes digging in the sand
Feeling the cool earth below
Moist, protected, free

A place for repose
Reading in the natural light
Breezes just enough to cool you down
An iced drink to satiate your senses
Letting go without a fight
Hoping you will not be found

Rearrange your schedule
So you can be in the flow
Take it slow
Soon you too will be in the know

That magical response
To your floundering in the dark
Is to get out and abound in nature
Jump aside

Take a big stride
Walk in the park
Until it gets dark

Free your mind
Healthy soul and body
Continue to roam
Until you make it home.

ENDINGS

Endings
Can it be that an ending always leads to a beginning?
Or does an ending signify just that, a succinct end?

Some things are meant to die out
Be complete
Disappear

While others are on a continuum
Keep going
And never leave
Even if you want them to

And still others have a circle
Die and renew
Regrow and break through
Wilt away, refresh and rebuild

Which one are you?
Are you too an end?
Or do you want to shed the tears
So new ones will invest in you
Get rid of the doldrums
Peel off the layers
And just like spring,
Rest and lay dormant,
So you too can come back rested and refreshed
Ready to take on the world again

Sometimes we are fragile
And require a bit of care
To reboot the juices within
And return to a normal rhythm
Allow this rest to happen
Make time for the renewal
That is why you bounce back
Able to shed the layers of life that weigh you down

Like a brand new circle
On which to continue
Creating a new path
For your life
And those you love
In order to move ahead through the muck
And give you that much needed push
So the pain will be a distant memory
Not erased in time
But smoothed over by the wind and rain
The tears and the sighs
Making the edges less sharp
The jaggedness less apparent

And the lines become connected
Creating a brand new cycle
A circle never-ending in time.

And when it is safe
You will leave your warm cocoon
And tentatively search for a pinprick of light
So you can soar through it all
High above the darkness
And reduce your stress levels tenfold

For this is when you know the end is near
The end you have been longing to break from
The kind that weighs you down tremendously
The thick bonds that need to sever
Never to return to your heart and soul
For the break cannot be undone
And this end will certainly not lead back to a beginning
This is a serious break
One that caused your life to change direction
One that took your soul on a search
For freedom
For clean air
For your fears to subside.

Some ends are meant for change
Change is inevitable and can be good
But change from integrity and the essence of who you are is never
good
And God would not want us to stray
Keep our soul energy intact
While you go down that path of trust
Kindness and transparency are key
Honest to your core
And everything will turn out for the best
Even if your best did not bring you here

Reach down to help another
But do not be pulled into their darkness
Stay above the ground
And do not falter from this path
For your end is not their end
And your beginning will not depend on theirs
But be cognizant of the gloom
Ride through the storm

Try to keep a bubble around your outer self
And a close watch on your inner self

Shed the parts that are no longer you
And watch as you
Renew
Regrow
And rejoice
So once again your ending will be complete
One that doesn't have to attach again
For spring comes after winter
And it does not take the old plants with it
Because spring does not need it
It instinctively knows how to create and grow and revive

And you too will learn this process
As you go in and out of your own hibernation
Sensing the parts that no longer matter
The ones that are holding you down
That are giving you a headache
Serving no purpose
Causing undue stress
Learn from it and let it go

The energy will be recycled and when it is shed
It will be turned into a greater purpose
One so great you will not miss it
Because you will be on your road to a new beginning
Allowing the love and warmth to shine through you
Creating a glow from within
Emanating into the heavens above
Guiding your ways
Keeping you healthy
Treading lightly so as not to miss out

On the moments
The peace
The here and now
The present
Ending a time
Beginning anew.

BREAKING IT DOWN

Breaking it Down
You can swim through it
Go around it
Climb over
Take it apart

But whatever you choose
There is more
It cannot be disintegrated
Nor can you ignore it
For it is so big
Like an iceberg

Chisel away in chunks
Until you need to rest
And wait
Until the hurt is diminishing
And a layer is created to protect

Heal from the inside
Play these games no more
Break it down
Into pieces and parts
For you
Until a design comes through

Feel the sudden release
A whoosh of breath
To let you know it is ok
An immediate lift of weights
Catapulting you up and over

If it is not high enough
Turn around and go back down
You will not stop until you hit the ground
Running through it
All the strength you have left

Give it freely
It will give back to you
Breaking it down
Little by little
Day by day
Play after play

It may not be right
But at least you tried
Figured out a way
What do you say?
It is a ginormous fight

Don't hide your sights
For up ahead
You will be met with battles
Scars forevermore
You may need to go out that door
Leave them lying on the cold hard floor

For thoughts can bring you
Back to now
You have won
It was fun
Take a bow

Reap the rewards
Quietly sit
See what fits
Let it flow
Take it slow

Be in charge
Of your mind
And you will find
With lots of strength
You will be
Breaking it down

A story is told
Lo and behold
Breaking it down
A newfound hope
Only you can see
Until you are free

Courage and wisdom
Come in time
Truly need to speak your mind
Even when the stakes are high
What is at the other end?
Perhaps there is a real friend

Breaking it down
In your heart
In your soul
In your mind
And you will seek
A way to defeat

The unkind, cruel
And helpless ones
All without a fight
Pick them up
And move along
So they will not bring you their song

Keep your armor on
Until you find a place
A glorious space
That envelops you
Peace returning
From within

Breaking it Down

SHEDDING

Shedding
Flowers fall to the ground
Shedding the old
Never looking down
Layers of yellow upon the ground
Returning to earth for yet another life cycle

Shedding the layers of life

BREAKTHROUGH IN THE CLOUDS

Breakthrough in the clouds
A hole that leads you to out
from nowhere
getting unstuck
buoyed by the fluffy clouds
they will take you there
and hold on
to God's might
Find the blue through the hole

EVERY TIME I TURN AROUND

Every time I turn around
Another day dawning
Another day coming
Restless, ready to start

Seize the day
Try to start
Find your own blessings in disguise
Mimic life
Even if you don't feel it

Go through the motions
Until they become habits
Let the sun shine through your skin
Absorbing the light
Let it emanate from above
Radiate to all angles

Take the warmth
The energy and sun
With you
To propel you forward

Don't look back
Try to find
A morsel on the ground
It will help you focus
To a new dimension

Then gather up your strength
And move around
Breaking through the layers
The stagnant layers
That needs rekindling
A warm fire within

Start small
With a smile
A nod of your head
A greeting
Look up
Out and around

Waiting for a sign
To continue this path
Grow and glow from within
Ready to shed
The old from the new
Keeping the old fresh and true

Moving in circles
As a straight path is sharp
A circuitous route is a must
For when you go back and forth
You will discover more things
And find more choices within

Allow it to unfold
Bringing sense to the gloom
A bridge to transition you there
Accept your choices
For they hold you true
Brings meaning to your life and spirit

God will throw you a net
Holes for the pain to drip through
Until you are nearly through
And the new you
Will build up and rise again

Helping the fears subside
Calming the nerves
Bringing gifts
A new confidence
Light and refreshed

Assisting you in every way possible
Hoping you catch the waves
See beyond the darkness
Bring in the sunshine
For health and wholeness
Makes up you.

LET THE RAIN FALL

Let the rain fall
  down upon your face
  lightly touching the ground.
Clearing the cobwebs
  of your soul
Cleansing the hate and anger
  in your heart.

Let the rain fall
  spattered and separate
  fighting the gravity

Your situation is no less
  Turning it around
  in your mind
Pushing back against the sound
  It is quite a mound
  Astounding actually.

Let the rain fall
  you can't catch it all
  letting it slip through
  your fingers

It will still renew you.

Sometimes to let the rain fall,
  Tears will be shed
  Things will be said
  And some things will die
  So please try

To renew and rebalance
And rebuild
Another level
Until you see
A way out.

Let the rain fall.
For if it is not free,
You will also see

The shedding of the spirit
Disentangled
Disembodied
Winding around and through
Intricate little corners
Touching the Earth

Playing with light
Wetting the ground
Not making a sound

Some will pitter-patter
as they fall
Nothing to do but watch

Pick yourself up and
do it with grace

Ease will come later

Shine once again.
Let the rain fall
So the sun can
come out again.

Drenching you in all its warmth.
Lifting you up again.
Onward
Glancing up at the sky
Thanking God…
    counting your blessings
    as raindrops scatter about

Knowing you cannot capture it all.
But revel in this moment
For that is all you have
Focusing on renewal
Bringing you back
    Rebalanced.
    Rebuilt once again.

For holes make you "whole."
You will see far with these holes.

And they will become
pieces of you,
which make you a complicated puzzle.

Each set in its own way
Some discarded
Some turned sideways
Even upside-down.

Get out of your own way

Play the pieces you have
    with kindness,
    with grace,
    with difficulty,
    some with ease

The holes are simply time
Moving through space

Let the rain fall
Don't capture it all
Grab the moments
Make them last
Breathe through it.

The journey of your "whole" life.

BETRAYAL

Betrayal
Be true to all
    NOT
Better show up
Come up short

Tramp them down
Throw them out
Waste
    NOT

See it all happening
before you
Stay true to yourself
Do what's right
Don't bother anyone.

Where does that get you?
Nowhere.
On the inside,
    managing the stress.
On the outside,
Treated like crap.

Use you up like a broken
    Cracker
Crumbs scattered
No need to sweep up
Their deed is done.

Anger rising to the surface

Tamp it down.
Try to fit it all in
    a small space
    ready to explode

The hypocrisy of it all
is killing me

Why don't people
stay true to themselves?

Why don't they tell
the truth?

Why do they continue to
cover up and stay neutral?

This is too much.

Is this too much to
ask for?
    Straight and honest.

Open and direct.
Preserve the guilt.
Say it like it is.
Don't throw others out
at your own expense.
Truly a disaster.
The ultimate betrayal.
A parent to child.
"Don't make me choose"
Words of the unwise

Push you aside like
garbage.
Continue to plow through.
Cutting holes, tunnels,
Chasms too deep to repair.
Learning that others don't
care.
You are expendable.
You are breakable.

You do not have any
strength left to
fight this battle.

You choose to be honest.
It gets you nowhere.
It crosses paths with
all the ones that
are in it for themselves.

The ultimate betrayal.

One that transforms
into an abomination
of oneself.

Never to be recognized
by any loved ones.

Gathering others on
their side, making
a team in numbers.

But, you, thrown
to the wayside,
hanging on.

No one thought you
could do it.
No one knew you
could hold on.
No one saw your
strength.

But you are fading fast.

For words are harmful.
And actions are worse.
They creep up inside
and tear you apart.
Finding you in pieces in a
heap.
Hard to get back up.

Tired of this old game.

Egos at stake.
 Selfish ways.
 Ultimate betrayal.

One looks up.
God is not watching.
He is not helping.
Not healing the hurt
 The anger
 The disconnect

Flying out on a limb to try
Something new.
  Break through the
  Clouds and dirt

Can't see it clearly
Find your inner strength.
Renew you.

Complete betrayal.
All alone.
Never to feel the connection
to family again.
The spirit is broken.
There is no hope.
  It is all used up.
Someone else's pain
  is their ultimate
  gain.
They relish in the fight.
Making it seem all right.

But God has turned a
blind eye.
He doesn't even see you
cry.
Complete Betrayal.

Lose it all now.
Thrown out to drown.
Stamp you down into
the ground.
Full of dirt.
It doesn't hurt.

Brush it off.
Clean out the wound
Quiet as can be.
They will do it again.

It is necessary.
      Ultimate betrayal.

Where to turn next?
Who to trust?
Really, it is all too much.

Place your hands on
your head.
Give in to the control.
See where it takes you.
To a dark place.
A place you don't believe in.

Surrender no more
March the other way.
Give it time.
It won't matter anyway.
There is no hope to heal.
Ultimate betrayal

Cut it out like cancer
And keep going
Leaving chunks of you
behind -- so you don't have to feel any longer.

Put together a new
and evolved you.
  No one cares.
  No one recognizes
    you anyway.

They are stuck in their
own world – in it for themselves.
Telling themselves it is
Ok to leave their
child behind.
And fill the space
with someone new.
Even if it is not
honest or making sense.
Some people find
themselves too late in life
and make excuses
for their bad behavior.
Thinking it is ok to
throw out people
to the wayside when
they no longer serve
your purpose.
But as truth be told,
This is the ultimate
betrayal.

Be true to all
but above all be true
to you. And if
you are left standing
and you are all alone,
at least you did it

with strength, care,
respect and honesty.

It doesn't make you
feel better to be
thrown out, trampled on and not loved.
In fact, it makes
you question your
values – your rights
as a human, a person that deserves
a space in the universe.
But if no one understands
then maybe it is time
to move on.
Some betrayals are
too big to comprehend.
Ultimately, it is up to
you. Care enough
about you to get
through.
For in the end, you
are alone and true.
But at least you are
through.

WATER UNDER THE BRIDGE

Water Under the Bridge
Keeps flowing
Dips down
Around the bend
Can't stop

Shatters the silence
Like crystal shards
Peeking out
Making room and crevices
for more water to flow through.

Hunker down
Until, the water is under the
    bridge
And you are free to go
Scraping your knee
It isn't pretty.

But if that is all you got
The hurt will heal

The flow of energy to your
heart will not
It pierces you
Stabs you in your dreams

Teaching you to go under
Turn around
Come back up for air on
    the other side

Water under the bridge
It doesn't matter anymore

...But it does...
    Teaching you to put
    one foot in front of the other
    Creeping along
    Finding a new path
    Evolving over time.

That endless trickle of hurt
    and pain and loneliness
Your heart is still beating
Covering up a mountain of
    blame.
Heart murmurs, slow it down
Barely breathing at times.

Sends you into a panic

One of fear?
    or
One of excitement?

That stop-start of water
under the bridge.
No longer.
Take control.

Let it out.
Poke a spot and let it
    drain.
Forget the blame
There is no shame.

Deflate and energize.
Grounding with Mother Earth.
It will "trip" you into feeling
    yourself momentarily

You exchange your energy
    to heal your pain.
The positive and negative ions
    cancel each other out.
Until you are one with the
    Universe.

You can ask for more.
It is expected.
Spare parts are available.
We all need a tune-up.

Water under the bridge
No more
It does still matter
Let it flow to the other side
And grab onto the rails.

Let it carry you out and over.
For balancing will become
easier.
And inside will match the
    outside.

One more round.
One more time.
Until at last
Your breath is jagged.
You do not care.

You can separate
Into a cloud of protection.

Only letting through
Those you knew.

Throwing the crystal shards
into the water once more
Making their rough edges
        smooth over time.
Diamonds of light
        stealing your sight.

Don't panic
Those shards will bring
        you to the surface
Coaxing you to hold on.

Pointing to a new direction.
A new face

Knowing that is all you
have to give.

Tried and true
That is the way.
A brighter spot to hang onto.

Fill your lungs with clean air.

Clear your head
A path will show up
And you will chance it

Throwing <u>nothing</u> to the
 wayside
For when you do,
  Your truth is shattered
  And nothing comes your
   way again.

Some things are meant
to teach you
While others tear you apart
Without any reason
Those are the ones to watch
 out for
The gouging out of hope
 and kindness
No longer room for respect
 and love

Those <u>others</u> finding any
 excuse for themselves
To be able to let you go

Thinking that is
 "Water Under The Bridge"

Well, that bridge is broken
A disastrous heap
Gaps everywhere

Too tired to catch up
Too exhausted to care
"Others" can take that
heap to the dump
It piles up everywhere.
Around them.

Water cannot flow.
Down and around the bend.
The debris is so deep
It keeps it from flowing

No grace
No thoughts
No sorry

You weren't going to get
that anyway.

So keep on trekking.
Like a diamond in the
     rough.
Loose, battered and
     Alone

Look no further.
The sun will shine down
     again.
Melting the pile of debris

Creating new parts
All untold.
Never to stray
Don't let them push you
     away.

Hunker down yet again
Until the water is under
     the bridge
Making your way
Until you are free to go.

It is your time to
morph into something
bigger.
You will not be thrown
away any longer
Swept up under the rug

Truth be told…
And your wings will grow.
Taking you to a new
    level
A new dimension
Where you will be found
And loved
Once more.

HURT

HURT
Heal Under Real Time
Heal Up Really Tight

A small pinch
A pain
A bigger pain
Until,
It bursts
Hurt.

Hitting until real tears
Flowing
Tearing you up inside
Making room for growth
Hurt.

Make amends now
So your hurts will heal.
Hiding until relevant twists
Take a stand
Turn it around
Hurt.

How do you tell?
Yelling, bursts like a damn
Move away quickly
Caring not
Hurt.

A dead end now
Calm your fears
Allow air to come inside
Deep breaths now
Hurt.

Why do others continue this mess?
Trying to understand
Just be honest
Solid as a rock,
Hurt.

Deep in doom
Gloomy,
Sick with pain
Searing inside
Hurt.

Dissolve it with silence
Be present for the pain
Endure it
Live it
Rake it through the coals
Hurt.

Bring it all together
Ooze it out of your body
Squeeze it out of your soul
Memories lie dormant
No more physical pain
Hurt.

Heal Up
Right Time

Make it work for you
Dampens your mood
Allow your spirit to soar
Grab on for the ride
Concentrate on what matters
You.

No more hurt
For now,
You are healing
From the inside out
Bringing forth your light
Effervescent with a sparkle

Shine to the heavens
Find your grace
In your place
Poised, balanced
Hanging up ridiculous troubles
Hurt.

Hinder no more
Plow ahead
Struggles are many
But continue to climb
Out of the darkness
Hurt.

Find a sliver of strength
Deep inside the hurt
Ready to explode like a hurricane
Swirling upward at immense speeds
Shooting out at every angle
Hurt.

It comes in bursts
Take advantage of its speed
For when you explode
The hurt dissolves
In tiny pieces
Easier to break up
Hurt.

Shards everywhere
No matter
It needed to be released
Like a damn shaking with fear
Do not let fear decide
Hurt.

Come and evaluate the damage
It won't cost any more
For it is dispersed
And the universe will extend
To absorb it all
Hurt.

Through the glass
There is a might
Let in the light
Feel the melding of the anger
With the damage caused
Hurt.

Then breathe out
One long sigh
A deeper breath
Carefully finding its way
Until it extinguishes the flames
Of hurt.

BALL OF FIRE

Ball of Fire
Rising up in my throat
No way out
Lodged
Stuck
Ready to explode
Help me to get it out
Move it along
Rise to the surface
Find its way out to the universe
Hang up any indifferences
Swallow your pride
Ask for help
It is so deep
Need counseling to coax it out
Safe environment
Kind words
No backstabbing
Trust again
No betrayals

Ball of Fire
Wanting to tell it like it is
Without judge, net
Without fear
Wisdom at its finest
Knowing it all matters
Keep on breathing
Contact no one
Disperse its energy
Pouring out its thick coating

Holding you back
Wanting to relate to others
Make a friend
Tell your story, your truth
And let it be heard

Ball of Fire
Asking you for its release
Again and again
Until you can breathe once again
Without any obstructions
Not wasting any air
Free flowing
Once again
With walls of armor to protect
No more betrayals
No more hurt
Go away
This Ball of Fire

TWO LONE TREES

Two Lone Trees
Poking through
Reaching high to the sky
Green with foliage
Soaking up the sun
Learning all they can
Every day this beauty exists
Swirling air currents through
The Two Lone Trees

Making their rounds until all are filled
With the presence of vitality and nutrients
Coursing through their centers
Expressing their boundless beauty
Equipped to give back to Mother Earth
Enriching the soil
Infusing it with love and care

Time matters
In fact it is of the essence

To continue their growth
Radiantly shining upward
Connecting the physical and spiritual realms
Earning their reward
Making their place known
Offering shade and comfort
A trunk to lean on
Proud and full of life
Two Lone Trees

PUZZLES

Life is a series of puzzles we put together

A BREAK IN THE CLOUDS

A Break in The Clouds
Swirling
Acquiescing
Grappling through

Pinprick of light
Finding its way
Settling in for the night
"Seek and ye shall find"

Making shapes only the mind's eye can see
Revealing something new every time
Transforming
Changing
Shedding
Particle picking up the pieces

White fluff all around
Maddening shapes and sounds
Angry clouds
Coming in faster and faster
Storming
Pelting you with rain

Relief now
All used up
Thrown away
Save it again for another day

Fluffy, buoyant opaque clouds
Traveling faster
Lots of places to go
All over the world

Squeezing their new path
Returning to a different part of the sky
Blue, luscious color showing through
Making your world a brighter place

Light seeping around its edges
Straight at you
Enticing you to look up
Soak it all in

Cycling its way to make your day
Lengthening its time for you to stay
Do you dare play?

Noticing the animals in the sky
Newness every time
Oh look, how time has flown!

Good thing the sun has gone to bed
Moonlight shows you the way

Your sleepy head
Hits the pillow
Wondering
Dreaming
Yearning
For another day
Revealing
The Break in the Clouds

All WAS BROKEN

All was broken
And lost
Deep down in the crevices of life
Defeated
Exhausted
Tired
Cramming it all in to a little space
No way to back out

Teeming with possibilities
To move forward
To get out
To go through
To crawl around
To press on
To go about your way

But…
All was broken
And lost
Life as I knew it no longer existed.
Thrown to the wayside
Done with me
Validation never needed
Simply love and time
Forgetting your roots
Can cause search and rescue
So extreme
That….
All is lost
And broken

Reminded once again that all roads lead to nowhere
Cannot control the other one's ego
Too much is missed -- time
No one to care -- love
Listen no more – lapsed

Lapsed into a world of control and manipulation
All was broken.
All was missed.
All will hurt.
All will be lost.

A TRUE FRIEND
Dedicated to Sue

A True Friend
Amazing and Comforting
Clear Trust
Never a betrayal
Small window of time to develop a friendship
Giving in to its love

One that does, acts and thinks with their <u>true self</u>!

Never to be thrown out like garbage
As if you never mattered in the first place
A true friend
Would never cause these hurtful things

"When you are proclaiming peace with your lips,
be careful to have it more fully in your heart." St. Francis of Assisi

TRUE FRIENDS
Dedicated to Phyllis

True Friends
Glimmering like a jewel

Ready when you are

Picks you up when you
 are down
Turns your frown
 upside down.

Pedicures, talks over coffee

Pasta, charcuterie,
 sweets and treats.

Helps you heal
 what a feat.

Talkative, silent
 just standing by
Observant, action-oriented
 ready to fly.

True Friends.
 Don't let it end.

Sun up, sun down
 True friends are
 always found.

No need to make a sound
True friends abound.

Waiting for you
Until the crying is through

But they would never poo-poo
The things that you do.

For emotions run rampant
In and out of your heart

Take a giant leap
You have to start

With hearts wide open
You need not fret

True friends will see
 that you always get

A hug
A smile
 Just stay awhile.
A sigh
A nod
 Comfort and care.

Energized now by your
 love
True friends imperceptibly
 wink and do not think
For some things are better
 left alone
Friends are <u>chosen</u>

Not a hard thing to do

Especially when I have…
　　YOU!

Thank you.

TIME AND DISTANCE

Time and Distance
    The heart of healing
Create more space
Minutes turn to hours
Closing the gap
Heavy with a sigh
Don't cry
    Will you do it all again?
Distance is needed
    Hear the rolling of the waves

The past has clearly passed.
History with no connection
No threads
Only time and distance.
    connecting to no one
    asking nothing
Uprooted again
Finding a shared space in
    which to heal.
Time and Distance
    seedlings will sprout
    finding something new
    growth will be good
    a new focus
    clear your mind
Let the moment take shape
    organically weaving its web
    caught in its clutches again.
    A tangled mess
    An imperfect world.

Fairness justified?
Constant bolts of lightning
Changing in an instant
Pack up your feelings and
     go again
Only to be shot down some more
Where will it go?
What will you be?

Feeling the fire burn within
Running on empty
Out of time and distance
No space to connect
     Windows show you the
     outside world.
Fear creeps in again.
Turn it around.
Show me the light.
Please make it right.
     Calm, my child
     You will show no one.
No one will understand.
This myriad of pinpricks of light
Send it out into the universe.
Sparks will fly.
Connect them with your eye.
It is all a mystery anyway.
Floating up to the ethers above
Connection is lost in space.

Only time and distance exists.
Where to go from here?
Time is running out.
Ready to carry on.

Sometimes distance is needed
    to get through.
    to get better
    to heal completely.
Closing the door to all who
    wander.
Stay lost –
You cannot help them all.
Cure not.
Hate not.
Buoyed up by your thoughts.
Creating a new space.
Be free.
Wander wide.
Come inside with me.

There is truth.
But beware.
Only fools believe it like you
For courage is miniscule
    in a thread of time.
Overpowering fear takes hold
moving in currents
rushing in
gusts of wind

Truth warms your soul.
Burns those who don't believe
Makes a hole in the empathetic

Protect yourself from all this
Celestial beings driven by their
    purpose
Finding out they are no longer
    loved or needed.

Time and distance
 Does it truly heal things?
 Or does it create a gap so wide
 you fall through and are
 forgotten?

Pick up your sights
Move on from it
Letting the chips fall where they may

There will be others who love you
Family is not real
 A thought
 a space in time
 someone to call your own.

You are not born this way
Family creates the chasms,
 the valleys,
The journey is yours to keep.
Savor <u>you</u> along the way.

You are your own family.
Notions of motions –
mindful untethering.
puzzles and rhythms of life
intertwining the good and the bad

Figuring out what to leave behind
in the created space
of time and distance

For surely in this heart of
healing,
there is a tree with branches
upon which to hang your
thoughts
    suspended carefully
    displayed for all to see
while you go to rest
just for some time and distance
    creating a whirlwind
    of rapturous thoughts
Your story lives
    hold on to it.
For unique as you are
connection can be followed
and even understood by a few
make that choice to let go
and be free
telling it like it is
allowing the branches to grow
playing havoc with the sun

Going off in various directions
Because family is on the run.
No need to cry anymore
Give them a shove out the door.

And know you will still be
found on the inside
Loved by a few.
Those that matter
And will not splatter
Every time you tell your
    story

No glory
No fame
Just a frame upon which
you base your morals
value the heart of you.
Through time --- and the
distance will no longer matter
It will be closed off to
        strangers peeking in

Gawk not.
Gossip not.
For in the end, you will have no
friends.

True as you are
Stay like a shooting star
You will go far
With your head held high
No more lies from the others
Especially your mother

As time and distance are
        created.
The love remains inside.
Dried up. Shriveled.
Waiting to fly.

TURN IT AROUND

Lurking
Creeping around the corner
Seen in every space

Only time will tell.

Figure it out tomorrow.

Burrowing
Behind my eye
In a tunnel.

Revealing
Space, sunshine, time

At a standstill.

Connecting
All the points of energy
In a never-ending circle

Peeking
Coming through in spurts

Listening
Electrifying silence
Conflicts abound deeply

Finding
Integrity is rare
Holding on to it

Trusting
Not everyone at face value
Deep within, knots exist
Scatter like dust when needed

Loving
Self, children, spouse
Care not
Kindness always
Deeply showing affection

Honesty always
Be a friend
Just a smile
Words of compassion
Vulnerable
Share a meal

Laughing
Telling stories
Hugs
Relaxing
Connecting again

Only time will tell

Your time
Your way
Take control

Grasp the wheel
Get on
Spin around
Have some fun
Adventure outside.

Nature abounds
Hummingbirds hover
Bees keep the peace
Connecting our food source.

Skipping, hopping, jumping
Swimming
Continuous flow of movement
Nature waits for no one.
Constantly changing,
     shedding, upgrading
Sunshine warms your skin
Takes it all in
Restful
Peaceful
Nutrients change your space

Shimmering
     upon the surface
     of the waves
Slowing down
     aging
     full circle
     passing the torch of light.

Capturing the energy
     points a mish-mash
     swirling to create some sense

of your life
roundabout ways

Delivering a spirit of love
    kindness
    compassion
    hurt
    wealth
    hope

People showing up
Finding
Nodding
Giving credit
    Too late
Where were they?
Why?
    Too bad.
Starting over.

FINDING HARMONY

Finding purpose…
> To love, to live, to be joyful, to have fun.
> All necessary to raise beautiful, strong children into intelligent adults.

Tell your stories.
> It is important.

Finding harmony in life…
> Balance…
> Living in life – not from the sidelines.
> Day trips to create more space in your mind
> A safe and comfortable home to keep always, come back to
> Jewels of friends
>> Trustworthy, kind, non-betraying types
>> Being able to freeform your conversations
>> Artful listening
>> Rambling on takes time and trust.
>>> Some are not meant to bother.

Friendships…
> Enjoying a hot cup of coffee
> Some nice tea
> A crisp glass of wine
> Some hearty meatballs
> Homemade sauce

Just be.

Listening…
> To the sounds of the world and air around you.
> The Great Lakes
> Adirondack Mountains
> Rocky Mountains
> Owls hooting

Blue jays cruising
Red robins laying eggs
Towering Oak, Maple
White Birch
Pine trees
Smell the forest
Hear the babbling brook
Creek splashing
Crayfish abound
 Explore around.
Sense the peacefulness
 surrounding you
  lost in time.

Alert, alert
 what's in the woods
 behind your house?
A predator, a peeker,
 a seeker.
Scream and run.
Let it be known.
Push on – trodding on the ground.
Moving fast.
Around the bend
Skipping rocks.
Splashes here and there
 a distraction
 Another direction.
Keep going
Out into the light.
Escape.
 Not followed anymore.
Sit at the park.
On the merry-go-round.
Snippets of views go fast.

Capture it all in a whoosh
of fresh air.

Breathe it in. Hurry.
Clean
    Unpolluted
    Cold air.

LOOKING BACK

Looking back.
It all sucked.
Sucked life out of me.
Sucked juices out of me.
Sucked the marrow out of me.
Sucked any possibilities out of me.
Sucked me dry.
Left me standing, no falling
    with nothing.
No pride, no ego, no time.
No love
No justice
    nothing.
No one cared.
Would I do it all again
    to conquer the truth?
No, I truly believe not.
No truth came out of truth.
No truth of mine was even believed.
Justice was not served.
You are just expected to move on.
Broken, perhaps dead inside and out.
Until a real friend,
    a non-betraying one
    actually comes to your side
    to hold you up.
To get you out of your stupor – your big black
    dark hole of hurt.
    Disappointment.
    Worries.
    Anxiety

Lack of sleep
More drugs for them to prescribe – always.
Sucks you dry.
Zombie-like trance
State of mind empty
Going on overdrive.
Into a dark abyss.

Then years later ---
finding a true friend.
    Rory
Creating a new life
Trying to leave it all behind.
Creeps up
    sinks in your pores

Giant leap of faith
    follow no one
Get the help you need

Heal into pieces
Whole self unlimited

Carving out the bad
Leaving it in the wells of darkness
Finding a sliver of light
Pulling up and out.

Creating a sense of worth
    again.
A purpose.

A Family – the greatest gift –
  Children.
  My own.

Finding lightness in my
    spirit again.
Herculean efforts of love
    and strength.
Trusting little by little.

Knowing there might be
    a God again.
One that hears me.
Hears my cries of hurt and
    pain.

Then another trauma hits
    Hard.
Muddle through.
Not working.
New way of life.
New way of seeing.
Come up for air.

Turn it all around
    in an instant.
Go back to your hole
    of despair.
Silence is your solace
No words of hurt
No raking over the coals
No sheets of armour
    needed.
Just love and time.

Not forgetting it all.
Just building a strong wall.

One that reaches to the ethers
out in space
    not defined
    fuzzy lines
Vulnerable no more
Respect the borders
Allowing space to breathe
Carry me on the wings
    of an angel

Those angelic creatures
    may hear me
    and save my soul
    from cracking open
    exposed to all
        hurtful people
    non-trusting
    nasty
    careless
    people
Until an angel patches you up
And creates tension
    waves of thread
    unable to loosen
    or pull apart
So you will be uplifted
once again
Into the ethers of heaven
and taken care of
    What a buoyant feeling
    Caring people

Loving
Transparent
Honest to a fault
Bringing you up and out
of the dungeons of death
purgatory at its best

But limbo no more
Stay connected
Stay in the light
    of love
    friendship
    and caring souls
Leave behind the dirt and dust
of your past and let it
grow cobwebs.

Search your soul and mind
for a new path.

Let it sink in
Create newness
    oneness
with your heart
    body and soul

Carefree
    fun
dance with joy

Leaving a tiny trail
    of footprints
    a small legacy to be
       treasured
    for your children
    to see you as a
    kind human being that
    was kicked around in life
    bowled over with pain
       and humiliation

But strength eventually
    ensued
Who cares about your
story – you are just one
of millions

Maybe <u>one</u> <u>will</u> find
comfort in your words,
your smile,
your gestures,
your actions

Put it out there
    carefully
so as not to get
kicked to the ground
    again

Wondering if it all matters
For in the end there are
so many stories
so many lies
so much gossip

You know who really helped
    you
Few and far between
All a crock
Weed out the unkind
Not much left, huh

A chuckle, a sigh, a nod,
a smile
    someone who is listening
    not haphazardly
    <u>not</u> with an agenda
       for wealth or fame
Not willing to play
    that ugly, nasty game.
20's came and went.
Up in smoke.
    Grabbing on for survival.
    Nothing was fair.
30's tentative, getting back
into the living again.

Blessed with children
Thank God.
Scared again.

How to teach them
that <u>not</u> all life is good.

But you must stand tall
and take a stance
on your honest thought
strength and adversity.

Through it all, you will
gain momentum.

Uphill battle for sure
But worth it in the end.

So – do it all over again –
    no – perhaps another
    day, another story,
    another way.

SOAPBOX

I know everyone has a soapbox
to get up on –
things they believe –
something they think they can change.
But what is it really?
A way to express yourself.
A way to preserve memories?
Finding a way to vent stress.
Stress can kill you,
I don't want it to kill me.

Jump down from this soapbox…
Into a pile of leaves
    the crunch
    the cushion
    the soft blow
How fun!
Relieve your tensions.

Wish I could find a pile here for fall.
What do kids do here?
Touch a cactus?
I need an oak, a maple,
a white birch, a pine tree –
All my favorites.
The smell,
    the stature,
      the love,
        the woodsiness.
Maybe I will have to roll down a grassy hill here,
not desert, not rocks, a hill with grass, real not fake.

Backyards are a safe haven from it all.
The chaos, the drugs, the riff-raff, the dishonest thugs.

Thank God for fresh air and nature.
Get down off your soapbox…
And live fully.
Express your right to live in this moment.

AN HONEST SOUL

Flowers abreast
    Flowing to freedom
    Ever vigilant

Capsized?
    Turn over
Retrace your steps
    Turn around
Not too far
    You'll get stuck
See into the distance
    Floating toward you

Help one soul.

Come into the light
See another perspective
Finding ground

Don't analyze it now.
Allow movement, breath, and colors
Just let it meld and be.

A path
    Little resistance on this one
    Ahh, a sigh of relief
Who's to know?
Who is to follow?

If you take the hard one
There are rocks not pebbles
Beneath your feet
    ground into the dirt
    scraping your soles

None are smoothed over by time.

Only time will tell

Kindness intersects this path
    Truth, integrity, trust.

Elements of love
Staring into the radiant stream
    of light
Grab it and move forward

Purpose is not grand
It just is
Find it. Small or big .
Who wonders?
Who measures?

Lit by the fire inside
    your soul.
    Forges ahead a path
    of strength

A mindset to be had by all
    No longer capsized
    nor upside down.

Climbing forth brings you
    into the light
    confidence abounds
    latch on to it
Where can it land you?
Bring your closest confidantes
You know the ones that
    truly care.
You never have to
    question.
Faith at its human finest.

Frailty no more
Rockin' side to side
Jump on this adventure
Ride it out to the shore

Dare to leap
A bridge connects you there

A piece of heaven
Sorts out your thoughts

Mumble jumble no more

Not a line – never straight
But zigs and zags
    that connect you.

Towards a greater path
Open up to the light
Refresh your soul.

Renew your mind.

Cleanse your heart.

Find some Fun.
Sending shock waves all around
Share this momentum
Bring your friends, your spouse.

No room for beggars
No room for depleted souls
No room for controlling freaks
No latching on to controlling thugs

Wrap around your
    stance
    your thoughts
onward and upward and out.

An innate ability to discern
    your best
To leave the rest
Unfairness goes far

True to your word

An honest soul.

TAPESTRY OF LIFE

Life is a series of struggles
Bits and pieces blown over,
    together, and through
Not cognizant of where
    it will go, what it will cause,
    nor who it will hurt!
You trudge along in your own
    world
Hoping to make a difference
Wondering who will help you
    along the way
If it is all worth it anyway.

Hang up your fears
Create a positive aura around
    you.
Change your thoughts

Love those who deserve it
Trust in the messy process of
    life.
Live fully, feel deeply,
    do what's right on the
    inside.
Create an unstoppable force
    within you.
Fire up your actions
Do what it takes.
Exhaust yourself no more
    with these negative
    intrusive people

Your actions will show your
    best side
Weave the qualities of
    you into your tapestry

Your life
Take control now.

FATE

Reverberation
>vibrate
>berate
>relate
Finite
>manipulate
Synesthete
>blending one's senses
Ringing out into space

Annihilate

Renegotiate

Signs of negotiate
>Belated
>Circulate
>Gravitate
>Master of your own <u>fate</u>
>Primate
>Final date
Magistrate
Heartbreak
Discombobulate
Pick your <u>mate</u>
>switch and <u>bait</u>
Close this gate
>on hate
>too late
Broken nation
Revelation

Damnation
Appreciate

    Close the Gate
    On Hate
    Too Late
    How does one Rate
    Sated in Fate

WAVES

Waves
    down and out
    around and through
Not at me
    in a circle
Waves
    surrounding me
    protecting me
Pulling the energy out
    to enjoy and sense this moment
Fulfilling your insides
    with your thoughts
    your blessings
    your gratitudes
Feeling the air in and out
    Fresh, crisp, clean
Cleansing you from the inside-out
    waiting for you to take action
    Be still
    Compassionate to oneself
Understanding that healing takes
    time
Live in the meantime
    Go forth and have fun.
Forget your fears.
Protect your heart.
Feed your soul.
    Come closer to God.
    Faith
    Happiness
    Love

These too will become real for you.
    Trust the process.
    Even if it lets you down.

Try. Try again.
Your love is endless.

Unbounded
Untethered
Floating on to ecstasy

Claim your space in the universe

Connecting to the spectacular
    moving energy around you

Floating on a cloud.
Dreaming once more.
Creating a sense of warmth
    glowing from the inside of you.

Find your passion
    and ignite it.
    Let it burn until it runs out.

Relight your loved one.
    Feel the flame
    Let it connect to your flame.
Two candles become one
    Stronger together
    Standing as one
    Holding each other up.

In this space and time
We call Earth.
    Allowing all our senses to
    ignite.
Go forth and have a say
    in your truth
        your life
        your fun
        your way.

MOMENTS OF FREEDOM

This moment
Your moment
Together as one with your soul's clock

Chaotic inside…
 Time wasted

State of calm…
 Creating moments of freedom

Allowing the space to breathe
 Even in between the stressors

Regrow the roses and stop to smell them
Your relationships enduring
 Mistiness flowing through
 Until there is no more veil.

The state of flow becomes you
Gratitude and gracefulness

This is your moment of freedom.

Being present to allow the
gifts of life to flow
through you.

This is time well spent.
Flowing moment to moment
All the while your awareness grows
And you do not let a moment
 pass you by
You grab on for the ride

Time ever present
Expanding to learn more
Moments of freedom

Look around you
The stillness talks
Speaking softly in your ear
     In a roundabout way
     Enticing you to play

Get out in nature to explore

You are the master of your own time
     Rhythms like no other
     Follow your breath
     Expand your horizons
And climb to the top of
your moment of freedom
          Light
          and
          Love
Finding truth in your way
A scattered path set out
     to explore
     criss-crossing until
     you reach the door

One that will open your
     mind
Helping you find
     moments like these
     together as you please
     To light the way – perhaps
you will stay and appreciate
your moments of freedom.

FEELING THE EXCAVATION

Excavate deep down
    In a cave, a well
    A deep space in your being
Allow yourself to feel it
    The sheer blackness
    The muddy, murkiness of it all
Swimming to the surface
    Through the garbage and debris
Getting stuck down under
    can't breathe, can't inhale
Exhale it all out
    Push it out
    Allow for new breath
Go in and chisel out more pieces
    It will take work
    Healing is a slow process.
Some pieces will float to the surface.
Allow it.
Do not resist it.
Other pieces will die and
    fall down.
Let them follow each other
      to the dark abyss below.
Still others will continue
    to pierce your heart
Making tiny holes so that
    plankton can
    gather around.
Patch this one and move on.

Sometimes the excavation is
    messy and morbid.
Other times it flings right off.
What freedom to see it fly away.
    Like a marble chunk in space.
    God will take that care away.

Chiseling, breaking off,
compartments unharmed
treasures found.
Hopefulness abounds again
Trust takes time.
    Time to build
    Walls crumbling down.
    You will not drown.
Be still and vulnerable
    protective yet safe in your shell.
Like a mermaid freely
    swimming below the surface.
Jewels glistening down below.
Some will stay buried
    Helping your soul to grow.
    Little by little these jewels
        get revealed.
The immense wealth of
knowledge glistens,
light cascading down
upon you.
Grasp on to the light.
Wear it as a blanket.
This will cross the
    barriers of time
excavating your soul
a little more.

Drowning out the bad
But leaving your soul
    intact.
It may have defects,
    but it listens
    it breathes, and it
    releases the old
Allowing the new to flow
    through
Traditions abound
    in this space
Feel the divine energy
    Taking over
Cleanse your soul
Excavating once again to a
    deeper layer,
A deeper level of understanding
Knowing all will not be as planned.
In fact, all will not
    turn out right.

What lesson is there in this?
    A whisper, a nudge
    Moving out of this hole

The chasm cannot be
     bridged.
So throw your energies
over another wall, another
hurdle.
Create a new bridge
The old one has gaps –
    too many misunderstandings.

Force your forward march
Trapeze over to the new one
Your true love will follow you
  Your children will not harm you.

A purging of sorts

An excavation so deep
  it is humbling

What will come out of this?
Clearly, someone will be
  left behind.
As long as you do not trample
  them, you cannot take
  the blame.

While others still ostracize you,
  you will wonder their
  mal-intent.
Urging you to give up
  give in to their
  demands
Oh no! You will not grow.
  Slowly, pull away
  from them.
Tease yourself up from the
  ground
or the depths below will
harm you and you will not be
  found

This is excavation at its
  finest

Wounds turned inward
sending messages of hurt,
anger and resentment
Gouge it out
And wisdom will spill forth
Conjuring up new images,
ways to play
space to create and breathe
    again
In which you are protected
once again, from the nastiness
of doubt, hatred and malicious
people – your own split
relations. No longer part of you.

The older generation
    will not get it
Stuck in their ways
Stubborn refusal to
    move on

Tethered to a string
    a cord so tightly
    wound
    It is choking,
    gagging
No need to be a part
    of this.
Brings you down

Focus anew.
Like Flowers blooming
Darkness subsides

A breath of fresh air
A breakthrough of light

A glimmer of sparkle
Dream, create your own
    soul's worth.
    your purpose is heard.
Let go of the controlling,
manipulative ones

And tie a knot so they
cannot crawl through.

Stay on this path of light
Understanding why will come
    someday.

Free your thoughts of resistance
A new pathway opens up

Cut that cord and
    fly away.

No harm done.
We all must move on
    Our life, our time,
    our way.

TIME STANDING STILL

Feel the breeze directed by time.
Coming in whispers
The steady but miniscule movement
    of the clouds
Speaking to you in the vast oneness
    of life.
Branches reaching out to the sky
    waving their messages in code
Flowers blooming open
    expanding to the possibilities
    their scent lingering in the crisp air
Birds chattering and tweeting
    landing aloft a ledge
Swings on the playground
    gently swaying to the breeze
Grasses shifting
    blades erect yet flexible
Rocks with their varying shades
    layered with strength
A meandering brook
    bubbling with laughter
A rogue bench isolated in its
    midst.
Take note and sit down.
Stay awhile in this moment of time.

Did you ever notice how time stands still
    when you wonder?
The curiosity of wonderment allows
    you to slow down
    and make a choice.

You are no longer racing
against the clock.
It is neither past nor future.
Just this moment.
No projections.
No judgements.
Just you in time standing still.

It's amazing, right.
Gather your thoughts in this
    expanded space.
Fill your lungs with air
Breathe in slowly and expand
        your senses.
Include it all.
Exhale deeply and slowly,
    forcing every last breath out.
Clear your mind.

Continue your curiosity.
The breeze keeps moving
    through space
Catching the molecules of
    your breath
Carrying these particles
    to a place in time
    where you can only imagine
    A mythical, healing
    calming presence taking over

And you feel the essence of life
    being renewed in you.
A peaceful, quiet nature
    like no other.

You are no longer racing
against the clock.
It is neither past nor future.
Just this moment.
No projections.
No judgements.
Just you in time standing still.

…Just you in time standing still.

RHYTHMS

Bask in your own rhythms.
This is your life.
    Happy and sad
    Kind and glad
    Down and out
    Figure this thing out.
Find your own flow.
    Fluidity, one motion leading into the next.
    Breath after breath
    Step after step
    Hiking up and down.
If your rhythm is halted,
    You do not feel.
    You do not like it.
    You try to change it.
    Resistance in its greatest form.
Flow haltingly comes to a stop.
Saving your energy to follow expectations.
Stop.
Change directions.
Pick up the flow again
Another time, another place,
    another space.
Follow your own natural rhythms,
It cannot be found anywhere else.
Look inside of you and listen to it.
Trust your intuitions.

This is your soul speaking to you.
    Loud and clear.
    Distinctly your voice.
    Open up your heart to this
        never-ending rhythm –
        a balance like no other.
Envelop yourself in this
    unexpected change of direction.
For you will be surprised how
    things will arise and tools
    to assist you on your
    understanding of the journey
    of your own life.
Let your rhythms flow.

ABOUT THE AUTHOR

This work is a collection of original poetry by Karen Langran. Her poetry is designed to allow others to feel and connect to the spirit of her words. Through her creative prose, she hopes to help others find hope in their tragedies and light at the end of the tunnel. She believes we are all luminous beings with a purpose.

"Let my burdens be lifted on the wings of an angel and be gone."

(Quote by Karen Langran)

Karen has always loved to write and has journaled since a young girl. Her motto is "When in doubt, writing gets it out." This is her second published poetry book. Her first poetry book is called *Split-Soul: Poetry from the Heart*.

Karen Langran was born and raised in Rochester, New York and now resides in Arizona with her family.

www.ingramcontent.com/pod-product-compliance
Lightning Source LLC
LaVergne TN
LVHW051642080426
835511LV00016B/2443